Let's Hear It For

Written by

Piper Welsh

rourkeeducationalmedia.com

*Scan for Related Titles
and Teacher Resources*

www.rourkeeducationalmedia.com

PHOTO CREDITS: Cover: © Kankaitom; Page 4: © elen; Page 5, 13, 20: © Nikolai Tsvetkov; Page 6: © Evgeniya Tubol; Page 7: © Wang Xiaomin; Page 8: © JPaget RFphotos; Page 9: © Tanirtak; Page 11: © epstock; Page 12: © Richard Jemmett; Page 14: © Marina Geraskina; Page 15: © Wikipedia; Page 17: © Lenka Dankova; Page 18: © Wavetop; Page 19: © raywoo; Page 21: © boyenigma; Page 22: © Vitalij Geraskin;

Edited by: Precious McKenzie

Cover design by: Renee Brady
Interior design by: Ashley Morgan

Library of Congress PCN Data

Welsh, Piper.
  Let's Hear It For Poodles / Piper Welsh.
    p. cm. -- (Dog Applause)
  Includes index.
  ISBN 978-1-62169-8708 (hardcover)
  ISBN 978-1-62169-7657 (softcover)
  ISBN 978-1-62169-9712 (e-Book)
Library of Congress Control Number: 2013936481

Also Available as:

ROURKE'S
e-Books

Rourke Educational Media
Printed in the United States of America,
North Mankato, Minnesota

Educational Media

rourkeeducationalmedia.com

customerservice@rourkeeducationalmedia.com • PO Box 643328 Vero Beach, Florida 32964

Table of Contents

Poodles are often pampered beauties of the dog world.

Poodles

Many people think Poodles are fancy, fluffy little dogs from France. Actually, Poodles are not always little, nor are they French!

Poodles come in three sizes: standard, miniature, and toy, the smallest variety. Miniature and Toy Poodles are quite small. But the Standard Poodle can weigh 65 pounds (29.5 kilograms). That's what many Golden and Labrador Retrievers weigh.

Miniature Poodle Facts

Weight:	26-30 pounds (12-14 kilograms)
Height:	11-15 inches (28-38 centimeters)
Country of Origin:	Germany, Central Europe
Life Span:	12-15 years

Purebred Poodles are entertaining dogs. There's a Poodle size for almost any home or dog lover. That's one reason Poodles are among the most popular dogs in North America.

The Poodle enjoys being a member of a loving family and tries its hardest to please its loved ones.

Poodle coats come in all different colors, including apricot.

The American Kennel Club (AKC) and Canadian Kennel Club (CKC) keep records of purebred dogs. In 2012, Poodles were ranked as the eighth most popular breed in the United States by the American Kennel Club.

Look at Me!

Poodles are one of the easiest dog **breeds** to pick out. Their coats are dense and curly wherever they're not shaved. The hair on Poodle feet, for instance, grows into tufts that look like snowballs. Poodle tails are **docked**, so they're short.

Poodles have slim, firm bodies from their hard-working **ancestors**. They have floppy ears and long, rather sharp **muzzles**.

Poodles do not shed much so they are the perfect dog for people with allergies.

History of the Poodle

The first Poodle-like dogs probably came from Asia. There they were used largely to herd sheep and goats. By the 1400s, they had been taken into Germany, Russia, France, and other European countries. The modern Poodle is probably most like its German ancestors.

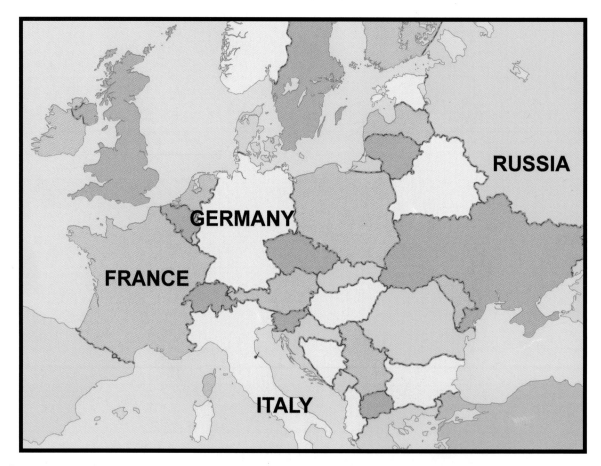

During the late 1700s, Poodles became extremely popular in the court of King Louis XVI of France.

Poodles love to water retrieve and used to do a lot of work in the water.

Among Poodle ancestors were many water-loving dogs with rough, curly coats. The English word poodle was borrowed from a German word, *pfudel*, which means to splash. Its French name, *caniche*, means duck dog.

The Poodle became a special favorite in France. Wealthy French women often owned Poodles. The Poodle eventually became the national dog of France.

Toy Poodle Facts

Weight:	14-16 pounds (6.5-7.5 kilograms)
Height:	8-10 inches (20-25 centimeters)
Country of Origin:	Germany, Central Europe
Life Span:	12-15 years

Miniature and Toy Poodles were developed by dog **breeders** from Standard Poodles. Breeders used the smallest standards as mothers and fathers. Over many years, the breeders developed smaller and smaller Poodles.

Toy and Miniature Poodles are very energetic, but also make great lap dogs.

Hunters still use Poodles to retrieve water fowl because of their love for swimming.

Poodles today are kept mostly as household pets. But Poodles in the past were trained to guide, guard, retrieve ducks, and perform in circuses.

Poodle Grooming

The Poodle's famous hair **clip** probably began during its water dog days. The coat was trimmed in places so that the dog could swim faster. But hair was left longer on the Poodle's chest for warmth in the water.

The practice of leaving tufts of hair on the Poodle's legs and tail probably began for circus shows. AKC dog shows today allow any of three different clips for adult Poodles.

The Continental Clip is a very popular style for Poodle owners to choose for their pets.

A Loyal Companion

Poodles are smart, playful, obedient, and friendly toward people. In fact, they need a great deal of human attention. Smaller Poodles, especially, have lots of energy.

When bored, Poodles can get creative and get into all sorts of mischief.

Poodles love to run around and go on daily walks with their owners.

Standard Poodles need more exercise time than smaller Poodles. Many standards, like their ancestors, love to swim and romp in woodlands.

Each dog of any breed has its own personality. But generally, Standard Poodles are calmer than their smaller cousins. All Poodles are alert and quick to bark, so they make good watchdogs.

Poodle hair requires plenty of care with a brush. Poodles shed in an unusual way. Most shed hair is caught in their curly coat rather than falling to the floor.

Standard Poodle Facts

Weight: 45-70 pounds (20.5-30 kilograms)
Height: 15 inches or above (38 centimeters or above)
Country of Origin: Germany, Central Europe
Life Span: 10-13 years

Poodles stay happy if given a lot of attention from the ones they love.

Doggie Advice

Puppies are cute and cuddly, but buying one should never be done without serious thought. Choosing the right breed of dog requires some homework. And remember that a dog will require more than love and great patience. It will require food, exercise, grooming, a warm, safe place to live, and medical care.

A dog can be your best friend, but you need to be its best friend, too. For more information about buying and owning a dog, contact the American Kennel Club at *www.akc.org/index.cfm* or the Canadian Kennel Club at *www.ckc.ca*.

Glossary

ancestors (AN-ses-tuhrz): those in the past from whom an animal has descended; direct relatives from the past

breeds (BREEDZ): particular kinds of domestic animals within a larger group, such as the Poodle breed within the dog group

breeders (BREE-duhrz): people who raise animals, such as dogs, and carefully choose the mothers and fathers for more dogs

clip (KLIP): any particular hair style

docked (DOKT): to have had an otherwise longer tail cut short

muzzles (MUZ-uhlz): the nose and jaws of animals; the snouts

purebred (PYOOR-bred): an animal of a single (pure) breed

Index

Websites to Visit

www.akc.org/breeds/poodle
www.dogbreedinfo.com/poodles.htm
www.poodleclubofamerica.org

Show What You Know

1. How many types, or sizes, of Poodles are there?
2. What is the average life span of a Standard Poodle?
3. Which Poodle needs more exercise, the Toy Poodle or the Standard Poodle?